All About Animals

Deer

By Christina Wilsdon

Reader's Digest Young Families

Contents

Chapter 1
A Deer Grows Up.. 5

Chapter 2
The Body of a Deer.. 13

Chapter 3
A Deer's Antlers.. 21

Chapter 4
A Deer's Year.. 29

Chapter 5
Deer in the World.. 37

Glossary
Wild Words.. 42

Index.. 44

Credits.. 45

Chapter 1
A Deer Grows Up

A fawn weighs from five to nine pounds when it is born.

The baby deer blinks as she looks at the world around her. She is only a few minutes old, so everything is brand-new to her. She sneezes as a blade of grass tickles her nose. Suddenly, something warm and wet washes over Baby Deer's face! It is her mother's tongue, busily scrubbing her from head to toe.

Mama Deer came to this quiet spot to give birth. Baby Deer is her first fawn, but she already knows how to take care of her. Mama Deer licks Baby Deer dry, then lies down next to her. Baby Deer nuzzles close and drinks her first meal of milk.

Soon Baby Deer struggles to her feet. She wobbles on her long legs. Mama Deer licks her with such energy that she nearly topples over. By the time she is an hour old, Baby Deer can walk. When she is about five hours old, she follows Mama Deer away from the place where she was born.

Doe, a Deer

A baby deer is called a fawn. Its mother is called a doe. Its father is called a buck.

7

Mama Deer leads Baby Deer to a grassy spot in the woods that has many leafy plants. There Baby Deer lies down, curls up in a ball, and flattens her ears against her neck. She blends in so well that she seems to disappear!

Mama Deer nuzzles Baby Deer and gives her a lick before stepping quietly away. She looks back once to make sure Baby Deer is safely hidden. Then Mama Deer heads off to find food.

Baby Deer naps. When she awakes, she looks around but stays still. Baby Deer knows that lying quietly is her best protection. A hungry animal passing by is less likely to notice Baby Deer if she doesn't move. She is also almost odorless! A fawn gives off no smells for a predator to sniff.

To keep her own smell from her fawn's hiding place, Mama Deer stays away from Baby Deer as much as possible. But she is always close enough to hear Baby Deer if she bleats or bawls. If a predator comes near, Mama Deer will lure it away from her fawn.

Mama Deer does visit her baby three or four times a day to feed her. Baby Deer leaps to her feet and nurses eagerly, wagging her tail the whole time. When Baby Deer is done feeding, Mama Deer makes her lie down again. If Baby Deer tries to follow, Mama Deer gently pushes her back to the ground with her hoof.

Hard to Spot!
A fawn's coat is dotted with about 300 white spots! In the woods, the spots make it more difficult for a predator to see the fawn, especially when the sun shines in between leaves.

Coats of the Seasons

White-tailed deer have summer and winter coats. Their coats change color so the deer will blend in better with the colors of their habitat. In summer the deer are red-brown, and in winter their coats turn either tan or gray.

One day, when Baby Deer is almost one month old, her mother does not make her lie still. Instead, when Mama Deer starts to walk away, she bleats softly. Baby Deer jumps to her feet and follows Mama Deer into the woods. Now Baby Deer travels everywhere with her mother. She tastes the leaves that Mama Deer eats.

Baby Deer also meets other deer for the first time. She sees a pair of fawns tagging after a doe. This doe is her grandmother! Baby Deer plays with the fawns while the does feed.

The fawns run and jump. They shove each other with their heads. They play tag. They chase butterflies and stamp their hooves at rabbits. Sometimes they jump right over each other!

Summer turns into fall. Baby Deer's coat is changing. Her white spots have worn away, and the color of her fur is turning from red-brown to gray. She eats only plants and no longer nurses.

Mama and Baby Deer stay together all winter. In the spring, Mama Deer chases Baby Deer away before giving birth to her second fawn. Later, in the summer, they pair up again. Baby Deer and Mama Deer will stay together for many years, separating only to have their babies.

Chapter 2
The Body of a Deer

High Jump

Deer can leap about 30 feet in just one bound and can jump over a fence 8 feet high!

The thin, long legs of deer are the perfect size and shape for running through woods and fields.

Leaping Legs!

If you were in the woods, standing still and alert, a white-tailed deer could sneak right past you with barely a sound! Its thin, long legs carefully and quietly tiptoe over roots and rocks. Its slim body slips between tree trunks. But if you move or make the slightest sound, the deer will race away in leaps and bounds.

A deer can run at speeds of up to 35 miles per hour for short distances — that's about as fast as a racehorse. When a deer runs on soft soil or through light snow, it leaves heart-shaped hoofprints behind.

The sharp hooves of white-tailed deer are used to kick and slash predators.

Big Deer, Little Deer

White-tailed male deer are larger and heavier than the females. White-tailed deer are also different sizes in different parts of North America. Deer in northern places are the largest. A northern buck weighs from 150 to 200 pounds — about the weight of an average North American man. A very big buck may weigh up to 300 pounds — about as much as a very, very big football player!

The smallest white-tailed deer live in a part of Florida called Big Pine Key. They are known as Key deer. A Key deer weighs about 70 pounds and is about the size of a German shepherd.

Sensing Danger

Deer use all their senses to detect danger. Animals such as wolves and cougars hunt them for food. Humans also hunt them.

Deer constantly listen for the slightest sounds. The size and shape of their ears help them hear faint sounds, just as cupping your hand behind your ear helps you hear better. A white-tailed deer can point one ear forward and the other one backward at the same time to hear sounds both ahead and behind. The snap of a twig is enough to send a deer bounding for cover.

A deer is especially quick to see motion. If you stand absolutely still, a deer might not notice you. But just one blink of your eye can cause the deer to run away! A deer's eyes sit high up on the sides of its head. With eyes in this position, a deer can see forward, backward, and to its sides!

A deer's sense of smell is also excellent. Its moist, black nose is like a glue trap for scents. A deer often sniffs the air while feeding to make sure no predators are close by. Deer also use their noses to smell which plants to eat.

Hightailing It!

A white-tailed deer's tail is as long as a twelve-inch ruler and fluffy white underneath. When a deer is frightened, it flips up its tail. The flash of white warns other deer of danger. The white of a doe's raised tail also helps her fawn follow her when there is little or no light.

A white-tailed deer can swivel its ears in all directions to listen for the slightest sounds of danger!

White-tailed deer eat up to 10 pounds of food per day!

Well-Chewed Cuds

White-tailed deer wander in woods and fields, eating the leaves of many plants as well as small stems, nuts, bark, grass, and fruit. Deer also like vegetables and fruits grown on farms. They will even visit people's gardens to eat flowers.

A white-tailed deer has no upper front teeth, but it has no problem nipping off leaves and twigs. It simply grabs them between its lower front teeth and a tough pad on its upper jaw. Then it chews the food off. You can tell that a deer may have fed on a bush if you find stems with ragged, chewed tips.

Food is crushed briefly between the deer's back teeth and quickly swallowed. Then it enters the first part of the deer's four-part stomach. Later, the deer coughs it up as a lump that is called a cud. It chews this cud thoroughly and swallows it again. Feeding this way lets a deer eat quickly while it is out in the open, where danger lurks. Afterward, when the deer feels safe and protected by its surroundings, it can relax while it chews.

The chewed cud then travels through the rest of the deer's digestive system. It can take up to one and a half days for a meal to be digested!

Favorite Food

Of all the foods that deer eat, they like apples best.

Chapter 3
A Deer's Antlers

Antlers or Horns?

Surprisingly, antlers and horns are not the same thing. Every winter antlers fall off, and new ones grow back in the spring. Horns remain on the animals.

This young buck has two points on each antler. This makes him a four-point buck. He is also known as a "Y buck," because each antler looks like the letter Y.

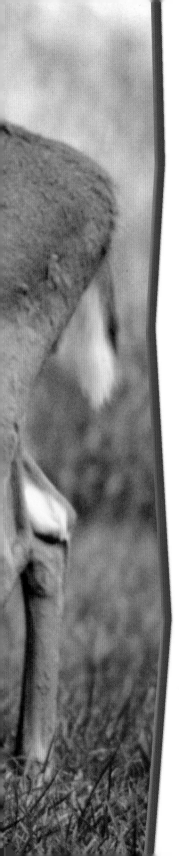

A Rack of Antlers

Every spring, bumps appear on the heads of white-tailed bucks. These bumps are the beginnings of antlers. They sprout from two knobs, called pedicles (pronounced *PEH-duh-culls*), that are part of the buck's head.

The antlers are made of solid bone, although at first they do not look shiny and smooth like bone. They are covered in a fuzzy skin called velvet. If you touched the antlers, they would feel warm, because the velvet is filled with blood vessels. The blood nourishes the antlers as they grow. The velvet stays on the antlers throughout the summer. By late August the antlers are fully grown. The velvet begins to dry up and fall off. The bucks help peel it off by rubbing their antlers on bushes and trees or sometimes by scraping the antlers with their hooves. Antlers can measure three feet across from tip to tip

A buck does not grow his first antlers until he is more than one year old. His first antlers are usually just single spikes. Each spike is up to five inches long. A buck like this is called a "spike buck." When he starts to grow antlers with more points, he will be called a "rack buck."

Wild Words

A **rack** *is a pair of antlers.*

Total Points

It is sometimes said that you can tell how old a buck is by counting how many points he has on his antlers. This is not true. Older bucks do have larger antlers and more points than young bucks. But the size of the antlers depends on the individual deer — what kind of deer he is, and if he has had enough food to eat. One buck grew antlers with 78 points!

Rack Attack

When a buck looks for mates in the fall, he is friendly to the does he meets. He is not as friendly to other bucks. When two bucks meet, the weaker one often leaves. If he does not, then the two bucks will probably fight.

First, the bucks look directly at each other and walk toward one another on stiff legs. The furry hairs stand up on their necks and backs. The bucks flatten back their ears and turn their heads this way and that to show off their antlers. They stab at bushes and paw the ground with their hooves. Then, heads lowered, they charge at each other.

Antlers crash. The two bucks push and shove with their heads. Each one twists his neck as he tries to flip his opponent onto his side. The battle usually ends with one buck giving up and running away.

Antler Drop

In midwinter the antlers of a buck fall off. First one drops, then the other. A buck with one antler usually will lose the other in a day or two. The buck then has two raw, red spots on his head, but they heal quickly.

The shed antlers do not go to waste. They are full of minerals, such as calcium, that animals' bodies need. They are soon eaten by chipmunks, mice, and other small creatures.

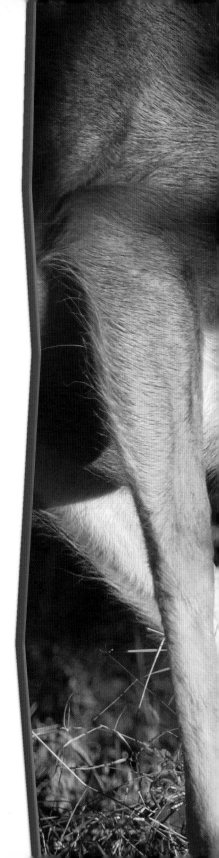

White-tailed bucks use their antlers to fight other white-tailed bucks for mates or territory, not to protect themselves from predators!

The mule deer looks a lot like a whitetail, but it has huge ears and a black-tipped tail. The branches of the mule deer's antlers divide into smaller branches with points. A whitetail's antlers each have one main branch with points.

The moose is the world's largest deer. It is about as big as a horse and weighs more than 1,000 pounds! The male's antlers are wide, flat, and huge.

Each antler of a male elk can be 5 feet long! Elk are also called wapiti (pronounced *waa-PEE-tee*) and live mainly in the Rocky Mountain states and southern Canada.

Different Deer Antlers

Deer antlers vary in size, shape, and design. Different kinds of deer grow different kinds of antlers, although many antlers have an overall similar shape. There are about 45 different species (kinds) of deer in the world!

Five species of deer, including the whitetail, are native to North America. This means their first ancestors were born here thousands of years ago and were not brought by settlers from other lands.

Unlike other members of the deer family, both male and female caribou (also known as reindeer) grow antlers. The male's antlers are bigger.

Caribou antlers have a shape that's a bit like the shape of a human hand, with a palm and fingers. Caribou live mainly in Alaska and Canada.

Chapter 4
A Deer's Year

A doe having her first fawn usually gives birth to just one baby. Older does usually have two fawns. Some does have three or four!

Spring and Summer

Spring brings new leaves and grass for deer to eat. The food grows just in time for the does, who are ready to give birth.

All winter, different families of does lived together as one big herd. Each family was made up of a doe, her daughters, and all their fawns. Now the oldest doe chases her family away. She needs to be alone for her fawn's birth. Her daughters will also give birth alone.

In summer, does and fawns form family groups again. The does eat while the fawns play. On hot days, they lie in the shade, panting like dogs. They are most active at dawn, dusk, and night.

The does watch out for danger. If a doe is alarmed, she snorts loudly and stamps one of her front hooves. This is a warning to other does, who instantly snap their heads up to look, listen, and sniff the air.

The bucks do not join the does. They form small bands made up of bucks only. They also spend spring and summer eating. Some of the food nourishes new antlers as they grow. The bucks often butt heads with one another, pushing each other with their antlers. For now, these shoving matches are partly for fun. They also help the bucks test to see who is strongest before the mating season begins.

Autumn

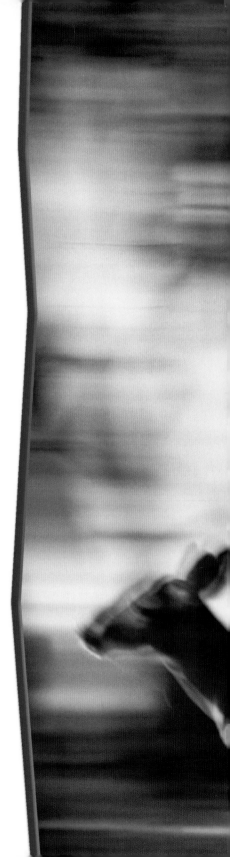

Autumn is a busy season for white-tailed deer. It is their mating season. It is also the does' last chance to fatten up for the winter.

By now, fawns have stopped nursing and are eating plants. They follow their mothers, nibbling on leaves and berries, twigs and stems. The deer also feed heavily on autumn crops of acorns and beechnuts.

The bucks, however, do not spend much time eating. They are too busy getting ready to find mates. The bands of bucks who have been friends all summer have split up. They no longer spar with each other. But a buck may still spar with a bush instead, hooking his antlers into its branches and stabbing at it from all sides.

A buck also rubs his antlers against trees as he travels through the woods in search of does. He is not rubbing the velvet off his antlers — that task is completed. He is rubbing his antlers on trees to mark them with his scent and to scratch off bark. This turns the tree into a signpost, warning other bucks that he is in the area. A signpost like this is called a "buck rub." He also scratches the ground with his hooves, making marks called scrapes. The does sniff the rubs and scrapes to find out about the bucks, too.

A doe will run away
from a buck until she
is ready to mate.

Stuck in the Muck

The size and shape of deer legs make it difficult for deer to walk in deep snow or mud. The deer sink and become stuck. If a deer falls on ice, it has trouble pulling itself up to a standing position on the slippery surface, just as you might!

In winter, bucks form their own small groups. They lose their antlers as well as their interest in does and fighting.

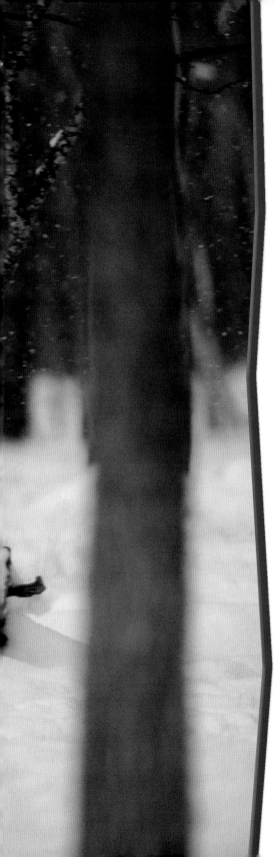

Winter

By winter, white-tailed deer have shed their red-brown coats. Now they wear thick, woolly winter coats of gray-brown or bluish gray. People sometimes say winter deer are "in the blue."

This thick coat slows down the loss of heat from the deer's body. It insulates the deer from the cold just as a down coat insulates a person. It does such a good job of holding in heat that if snow falls on a deer's back, the flakes do not melt!

Heavy snow blankets the land in the most northern places where white-tailed deer live. Winter in these places makes life hard for deer. They have difficulty traveling in the deep snow. Food is scarce.

One way does and fawns survive the winter is by forming large herds in sheltered places, such as woodlands. This is called "yarding up." The deer stay together in the yard for protection from wind and snow. They leave the yard to find food. The coming and going of many sets of hooves stamps out paths through the snow that lead to patches of food.

If the winter is very severe, deer may find only bark and evergreen needles to eat. If necessary, deer will stand on their hind legs to reach twigs, bark, and needles high up on trees.

Chapter 5
Deer in the World

The Best Habitat

White-tailed deer can survive in different habitats — forests, fields, and swamps. But the best habitat for whitetails is a place with both fields and woods. There they can feed in the fields and run to the woods for safety.

Where White-Tailed Deer Live

North America

The **green** area shows where white-tailed deer live today.

White-tailed deer are one of the most common big land mammals in North America. They live almost everywhere in the United States (except Hawaii, Alaska, and parts of the Southwest) and across southern Canada. Whitetails also live in Central America and parts of South America.

The Future of Deer

Although North America was once home to almost 40 million deer, there were fewer than 500,000 left by the early 1900s. Now there are about 20 million white-tailed deer, thanks to laws that control deer hunting. In some places, there are so many whitetails that people think they are pests.

Today, keeping deer populations at a good level means keeping their habitats healthy. In some areas, this can be done by setting aside and preserving their habitats. In other places, it means controlling the number of deer that live there.

Fast Facts About White-Tailed Deer

Scientific name	*Odocoileus virginianus*
Class	Mammals
Order	Artiodactyla
Size	Males up to 7 feet, not including tail Females up to 5½ feet, not including tail
Weight	Males to 300 pounds Females to 200 pounds
Life span	2 to10 years in the wild 20 years in captivity
Habitat:	Woods, fields, swamps
Top speed	35 miles per hour

You Can Help!
Become a member of a conservation group that works to protect deer habitats. It may even be your local zoo.

Glossary of Wild Words

antlers   the bony structures that grow from the head of male deer

buck   a male deer

buck rub   a tree marked by a male deer with scent and scratch marks from its antlers

conservation   the protection and preservation of land, animals, plants, and other natural resources

cud   a ball of partly chewed plant food coughed up by a deer for more chewing

doe   a female deer

fawn   a baby deer

genus   a large category of related plants or animals consisting of smaller groups (species) of closely related plants or animals

habitat	the natural environment where an animal or plant lives	**spar**	to practice fighting without harming the opponent
pedicles	knobs on a male deer's head from which antlers grow	**species**	a group of living things that are the same in many ways
predator	an animal that hunts and eats other animals to survive	**rack**	a pair of antlers
		range	the places where a species lives
prey	animals that are hunted by other animals for food	**velvet**	fuzzy skin that covers a male deer's growing antlers

Index

A

antlers, 22, 23, 24, 25, 26, 27, 31, 32
autumn, 24, 32

B

baby deer, 6, 7
birth, 7, 30, 31
bucks, 7, 22, 23, 24, 25, 31, 32, 34

C

camouflage, 8
caribou, 27
color, 8, 11, 35
communication, 8, 10, 31, 32

D

danger, 16, 17, 31
digestive system, 19
does, 7, 11, 30, 31, 32, 33, 35

E

ears, 16, 17, 26
eating, 8, 11, 18, 19, 32, 35
elk, 27
eyes, 16

F

fawns, 6, 7, 8, 10, 11, 30, 35
female deer, 7, 15, 27, 40
fighting, 25, 31, 32
food, 18, 19, 32, 35

G

group behavior, 11, 31, 35

H

habitats, 15, 26, 27, 38, 39, 40, 41
hooves, 15, 31, 32
hunting, 40

K

Key deer, 15

L

legs, 14, 15, 34
life span, 40

M

male deer, 7, 15, 40
mating, 32, 33
moose, 26
mother deer, 7, 8, 11
movement, 11, 14, 15, 16, 34
mule deer, 26

O

odor, 8

P

pedicles, 23
playing, 11
points, 22, 23, 26
populations, 40
predators, 8, 15, 16

R

rack, 23
reindeer, 27

S

size, 15, 26, 40
smell, 16
sounds, 8, 11
speed, 15, 40
spring, 11, 22, 23, 31
stomach, 19
summer, 11, 23, 31

T

tail, 16, 26
teeth, 19

V

velvet, 23

W

wapiti, 27
weight, 6, 15, 26, 40
white-tailed deer, 15, 38, 39, 40
winter, 24, 34, 35